Counterfeit Depression, Sweet Dreams and Finding Your JOY

by
Peter B. Holz

The National Suicide Prevention Line
1-800-273-8255

If you prefer to chat with them, search "suicide hotline" and you can find a live link there,
every day, day or night.

Other Books by Peter B. Holz
Who Built the Birdhouse? By Grandpa Pete
If You Could Make Frogs? By Grandpa Pete

© Copyright 2020 – Peter B. Holz
All rights reserved. This book is protected by the copyright laws of the United States of America. This book may not be copied or reprinted for commercial gain or profit. The use of short quotations or occasional page copying for personal study or reference is permitted and encouraged.

All Scripture quotations, unless otherwise indicated, are taken from the Holy Bible, New International Version®, NIV®. Copyright ©1973, 1978, 1984, 2011 by Biblica, Inc.™ Used by permission of Zondervan. All rights reserved worldwide. www.zondervan.com. The "NIV" and "New International Version" are trademarks registered in the United States Patent and Trademark Office by Biblica, Inc.™

TABLE OF CONTENTS

FORWARD	i.
DISCLAIMERS	iii
1. WHAT DOES DEPRESSION FEEL LIKE?	1
2. COUNTERFEIT DEPRESSION	3
3. YOUR BEST MEMORIES	15
4. ALL OF THAT FOR KIDS	23
5. SWEET DREAMS	27
6. FINDING A GREAT FRIEND	35
7. FEAR – THE OPPOSITE OF FAITH	41
8. COMFORT AND SECURITY	44
9. FINDING JOY	49
CUTOUTS	56

FORWARD
Monday, June 1, 2020

I don't know about you, but watching the constant crisis and riots on the news is making me wonder when this world went totally nuts. We are watching and listening to people freaking out, losing their jobs, ranting politically and having no joy, no smiles, and diminishing hope. There is fear everywhere, especially with kids who don't understand what is going on; why they can't go to school and wondering if they will this fall and having no way to deal with this fear. Add to all the economic ruin and racial unrest – depression and suicide. This is serious.

The good news is that there is hope and you can have joy again...even if you never had it in the first place.

I've been sad and lost hope. I have discovered that there are many things that can trigger what we like to call depression. Yes, there might be some problem in your brain or something awful in your past, I understand that. I probably can't help you with those things. If you have thoughts of hurting yourself or others, please call your doctor.

Those who know me can tell you that I do not have a rock-solid personality and I blame the real and counterfeit feelings that still mess with me. My apologies.

Here is the good news:

You might be feeling something else!

And I found some ways to deal with those counterfeit emotions. Once you deal with that, you can work on finding JOY and Joy that lasts!

Onward!
Peter, Pete, Paw, Grandpa Pete, Uncle Pete

DISCLAIMER

I am not a doctor, psychologist or psychiatrist. I am not a PhD and I have not spent hours studying what I put in this book. I have spent years observing these things and found myself "depressed" more days than not, until I realized that what I was feeling were emotions trying to make me feel depressed. I'm pretty sure those feelings are partly to blame for my divorce. I took a lot of notes over the past 30 years and it's finally time to put it all on paper.

I'm a Christian. **If you are not a Christian, please keep reading. Push on through this book. Look, if you have a problem and have tried everything else, why not try God?** I think this book can help you. The principles in this book apply to anybody. If you are a Christian, don't feel bad for having feelings; God made emotions, but we often get things confused…because we are not God. We don't understand everything and never will. Only God has it all figured out.

Some people claim that you are the sum of your decisions or that if you don't like your life, change it. I call BS on those theories. Some decisions are thrust upon you like sickness, death, accidents and divorce. Some parts of your life are not easy to change, and if you are more than 5 years old, you have responsibilities that you have taken on that need to be honored. I would never advise anybody to end their marriage and move to the Bahamas. You can get rid of the depression or counterfeit depression and find joy no matter your circumstances.

Stuff happens, you know? To everybody. It's just life. And the current news will soon be yesterday's news and it will then be something else to steal your JOY. And thankfully, you can use the strategies in this book to keep your Joy for the next attack. So, let's go.

CHAPTER ONE
WHAT DOES DEPRESSION FEEL LIKE?

First, I want you to think about what depression feels like for you. Go ahead, write down some words right here. On the next page I'll write my ideas but take the time to do this.

Let me reword this – *what does it actually FEEL like?* Not things that you think about or thoughts that go through your head when you are "depressed" – what does it feel like?

- I'm tired like I didn't get enough sleep.

- I can't concentrate or think clearly.

- My mind is in a fog or I feel like I'm in a dream.

- I have no interest in anything.

- Nothing makes me happy and I'm sad, angry or irritable, or all three.

- I want to put my head on my desk and shut everybody out.

- I want to sit in this bathroom and cry until I can't cry anymore. A deep down from my gut sadness.

- I wonder if I'm having a nervous breakdown.

- I'm so angry I can't see straight.

- I'm sometimes a grump, even to those I love most.

CHAPTER TWO
COUNTERFEIT DEPRESSION

But what if those feelings are counterfeit feelings? Feelings you *can* brush off or deal with?

When I feel depressed, I try to remember to stop feeling sorry for myself and really think about what is going on presently in my life. Once I do, I can snap out of it.
In other words, I need to make the decision in my own head to choose to think about something else – or get up and put into place a solution for the counterfeit depression attacking me.

> When you flip through the book, you will notice that counterfeit depression is only a part of the book. The next section is how to memorize your best moments. How is that related and what does Jesus have to do with anything? Please, just keep reading and it will all make sense, even if you can't imagine how right now. Please read all of it.

Here we go, in no particular order.

Are you depressed?...

Or are you sleepy?
Think about it. That fog you get; doesn't that feel a lot like depression? Did you stay up late or get up early? See Chapter Five for my tricks to fall asleep fast.

Solution – get a cup of coffee or one of those 5-hour energy shots. Best solution - take a nap. If that's not possible, tell yourself, "oh, I'm just sleepy, not depressed, I'm fine" and you should partly snap out of it. Force yourself to smile, put on some music, and take a break.

Long term – get some exercise every day, even if it's just a walk around the block or going up and down some stairs a bunch of times. Cut back on sugar, eat better. Oh yeah and turn off the TV and go to bed early tonight.

Or are you sick?
Do you have a cold or flu in early phases? Go take some medicine if that is your thing, drink some water, and go to bed early tonight. If it's something worse, get help for that, but it's not depression and it's not a reason to hurt yourself.

Or are you medicated?
Many over the counter medications, such as ones we might take for a cold or flu, have side effects including drowsiness. You know, the ones that advise you not to drive while using. Prescriptions also have side effects that you may not be aware of. If you often experience "brain fog" during the day, talk to your doctor about what you are experiencing so he/she can adjust or change your medication.

Or have you been drinking?
We've all heard that alcohol is a depressant. Now remember, I'm not a doctor, but I've been drunk, and I've seen the way different people handle booze. I had a friend who would get all sloppy lovey-dovey, everybody was his friend, he loved everybody, and everybody was just the best. I also had a roommate who just wanted to fight everybody. But I would get depressed, not happy. So, it was the booze, not something else.

I even find that a glass of wine will take me down, so I stay away from that. Obviously, this book can't fix a lot of things, I'm just saying, if you get "depressed" after drinking alcohol, dump it down the drain and avoid it or get counseling; it's not going to bring you joy.

Or is it jetlag or Daylight Saving Time?

Both of those time changes really mess me up, but that tiredness is not depression, and your body will adjust in a few days. Before you take a trip through time zones, do some research and get some tips on what helps.

Or are you dehydrated?

That's right. Maybe you just need a drink of water. I get headaches when I'm dehydrated, but it can really mess up your moods too. Seriously, go get a drink of water. If you "don't like water" maybe your water is bad, or you've been so used to drinking sweetened drinks it is just boring to you. Either way, your body needs water. Squeeze a lemon slice into it or get some vitamin water or something, just get water.

Or is this a 3pm slump?

This happens all the time to me. I have a big lunch then go back to work and then start to fall asleep (which can also feel like depression, right?)

Take a break, stretch, drink a glass of water, take a walk around the building and get some sunshine. If you live in a city with very little sunshine, at least open a window. Tomorrow don't eat so much at lunch.

Or are you feeling grief?

Peace be with you. There are books and books written about how to handle grief, but it is different for everybody. People who have not been through it have no idea how painful it is, so don't get upset when they say they understand, they just don't know what to say.

There are several phases to grief, and they don't happen in the same order for everybody. Put a time limit on grief, then start living again.

If you find yourself stuck in one of the phases, find a grief counselor to talk with.

I suggest you say out loud three times, "I trust you LORD, I trust you LORD, I trust you LORD." Talk to friends, tell people who offer to help specifically what you need done (they don't know), like the laundry or sitting with the kids or getting your groceries. If you are not up to going into public, don't go.

Or are you not sleeping well?

If you snore, you might have sleep apnea or it could be something else that a doctor can take care of for you.

There are good tips in this book that will help you sleep and give you comfort.

Or are you watching too much news?
Especially with demonstrations, both peaceful and violent going on from coast to coast. Add to that the political divisions? Those two things alone will wreck your thought life. Just turn that news off. I know you need to be informed but really, do you? Sure, you need to be educated on the issues so you can have an intelligent conversation and vote wisely, but if you are just feeding on bad news all the time, it's bound to bring you down and ruin your joy and peace.

Or are you constipated?
I'm talking about your "gut health." At least for me, I've found my state of mind is directly related to my grumpiness. Drink more water, get more exercise, cut back on cheese, and talk to your doctor. It could be that a prescription you are on needs to be adjusted or something else needs to be tried. Get regular! I even noticed that after my Dad had a big section of his gut taken out his mood changed for about a year. It was not a good time in his life, or ours either.

Or are you bored?
Think about it. Doesn't being bored feel a lot like depression? Go back to your list of what it feels like. Nothing is interesting; it feels like there is nothing to do. There are lots of ways out of boredom, and we both know that as soon as you get un-bored you could make a list of a hundred things you want or need to do. So, make a list of things you need to do. Not everybody is big on lists but do it anyway – when you are NOT bored.

If boredom is a problem with you or your kids, my best advice is to stay busy.

Stay busy.

Yes, you can still relax and read a book or take a nap but find things that you can do to serve others, give to others, be helpful, those kinds of things. Try it.

Or did you just come back from vacation?

If you just got back from Cedar Point or someplace really fun, the world will seem, well, boring by comparison. Even realizing that this is the problem, not depression, helps for me.

I'll talk about how to memorize the really, really good times in your life and use those good memories to help you fall asleep faster in another chapter.

Or is your blood sugar out of balance?

According to the National Institute of Diabetes and Digestive Kidney Diseases (NIDDK), our bodies are typically pretty good at keeping our blood sugar in perfect balance. In people with diabetes or pre-diabetes, high blood sugar can make you fatigued. Even mild and normal blood sugar fluctuations can trigger fatigue after you consume a large amount of simple carbohydrates, like sugar. This would be another reason to visit your doctor.

Or are you lonely?

This is a big one for a lot of people, even those with a spouse, friends, family and a bunch of loving kids. Or rebellious, strong willed kids. Or if you are single, divorced, widowed or just don't get along with any of your roommates, including your significant other, of course.

There are a lot of lonely mothers out there just trying to make it through another day. There is a group called Mother of Pre-Schoolers (MOPS) that is a great support group. Find somebody who can be in a play group so you can take a break once in a while. With the COVID-19 thing and school closures we are all having to be home schoolers; not everyone is cut out to teach, so that adds more stress.

Best advice? Get a dog, a cat, a fish or a bird. This probably explains why all the animal shelters are empty right now. There is something very therapeutic about caring for an animal and receiving their unconditional love in return.

Here is a less expensive idea – hang up a birdfeeder and take care of them. If you can't even to do that, go to the park and feed the birds. Or volunteer at a hospital or a homeless shelter. There is just something about helping others that takes away loneliness.

Other advice? Call a friend, chat with a friend, text a friend. Write a letter or email to an old friend. Think of somebody you can encourage. Buy five cards and send them to people that made a difference in your life. Send a note to wish somebody "happy birthday" or a note for somebody to "get well soon."

People need people, and that's the biggest lesson from the "self-quarantine" lockdown. If you need people, learn to FaceTime, Zoom or another app so you can speak face to face.

Or do you just hate your job?

Ugh, it can be such a struggle getting out of bed every morning and taking it minute by minute. I've had bad jobs too and I've been yelled at and called names and all that crap.

Let me tell you a true story. A friend was taking a break from his job at Walmart, sitting outside on a bench and he noticed a guy getting gas for his truck and boat – on a Tuesday. He finally realized that he was doing something wrong. He went back to school during the evening and was able to quit his job and start his own flavored popcorn business. He now has two stores and found a way to package it to keep it fresh for a year and sells online all over the world. He found his way to go boating on Tuesdays.

A boring job is not an excuse to go drinking after work or kick the dog. A rotten job might be the only one you can get for a hundred reasons. Or maybe you don't even have a job. Maybe you need to take your family and move to a city where there are better jobs.

Or do you have regrets that are making you sad?

Regrets can certainly drag you down. You know what I mean. The best way to break out is by giving thanks for what you DO have!

Or are you unemployed?

It stinks. I know how that messes with your self-esteem.

This is a tough time in your life; try to learn something from this. Do you need to downsize to a smaller house, take a Dave Ramsey course and get debt free, or spend more time with family?

If at all possible, use the time to learn a new trade, to increase your worth to your company or to finally start your own business—but that's another book. I am constantly amazed at the interesting, profitable careers that my guidance counselor never told me about. Of course, most of them were not even in existence in the 70's. It is entirely possible to make good money doing about anything these days. I had a guy offer to clean my dryer vent. How much demand for that could there be?

You can usually get free advice for the permits, book keeping, taxes, licenses, marketing and the ins and outs of running your own business from the Chamber of Commerce, City Hall, Facebook, YouTube. It's hard work but totally worth it for the Tuesdays you can be laying on the beach while making money.

Or is it soul unrest?

Stay with me on this one because I think this is the most common cause of counterfeit depression. Once you learn to deal with this, life will get better.

What do I mean by "soul unrest"? You know that feeling you get when somebody chews you out? Maybe it's something as simple as when you pull into a parking space and you get out and somebody calls you a jerk for taking "their" spot. You didn't do it intentionally; you just didn't notice them heading for it too. Completely innocent, yet it leaves you with a feeling you don't like and maybe even sticks with you for a while. *That* feeling.

Maybe the feeling that describes "soul unrest" is worse, like when you call someone a jerk or say something that hurts somebody else.

Soul unrest is part of the deal when you have an addiction. Whether it is alcohol, porn, prescription or other drugs, lust or an addiction to things, shoes, clothes or shopping, it is never enough; no matter how much you try, the addiction will steal your joy and bring guilt every time.

Whatever you want to call it, it is not peace and it certainly is not JOY. That's what I'm trying to help you find in this book!

If you get nothing else out of this book, please take this away:

GUARD YOUR PEACE
I didn't make up this phrase, but it comes back to me often. A few weeks ago, we had to leave our suitcases for somebody to take to the room and it started to rain and one of the soft bags got wet. We could have made a big stink about it and been angry that our stuff got wet or we could have guarded our peace, dried off our stuff, and moved on. Those are choices you make when the vending machine doesn't give you your candy or when somebody steps on your foot. Please, GUARD YOUR PEACE!

Or are you having a really, really bad day?

We all have them, but some days really stink. I spent four hours with tech support last week trying to get my email and website straightened out. That was so stressful to me I wanted to go jump in Lake Michigan, and it's just above freezing.

Here is the good news about a horrible day:

Tomorrow MUST be better! It's mathematically provable. And, **THE THIRD DAY WILL BE AWESOME**. If you have a bad day on Friday, Saturday will be better, and Sunday will be great.

CHAPTER THREE
YOUR BEST MEMORIES

Why am I putting this chapter in? This chapter will help you fall asleep quickly, but more importantly, it will give you something positive to think about when your world is crashing.

One of the best tips for dealing with depression, anxiety, pain, stress, hard times and difficulty falling asleep is related to the best days in your life.

What would you consider the best day in your life? Maybe not even the best *day*, think of the best 15 minutes in your life. Maybe it was the day you met the love of your life. Or perhaps a classic football play in high school. Was it a vacation you took? Was it watching your kids play a game on the rug in the living room or the time you first held one of your kids? Was it a first kiss or an awesome sunset?

Write down a *short* description of your best time here:

Now I want to help you think about that best time for about 15 minutes and consider this something to remember the next time you are in a place or situation that is especially perfect.

Memorize a memory.

That's the tip, memorize the memory. Memorize the moment. Observe all of your senses to lock that scene into your brain. Let this event be something nobody can take away. Something nobody can ever capture in a photograph.

Take your time to notice:

1. The sights – what objects do you see? Look at the bubble you are in – up, down, around, near, far, everything you can see. Memorize the colors, textures, patterns and movement of objects and try to imagine what everything you see feels like, sounds like and smells like.

2. The smell – what do you smell? Can you smell the sand or the ocean? Can you smell fresh cut grass or exhaust fumes? Can you smell perfume or cologne? Can you smell your drink or food?

3. The sounds – what do you hear around you? A song – what song? Birds? Cars in the distance? Wind in the trees? Kids playing? People talking? Dishes rattling? Listen closely and listen distantly. Can you hear the bubbles in your drink popping? Did you hear a plane fly over or a bus drive by?

4. The touch – can you feel a cold drink in your hand? Can you feel a breeze on your face? Can you feel the sun on your skin or the cool water on your skin?

5. The taste – what do you taste? Can you taste the apple you are eating or the drink you are holding? Describe it.

6. Deeper memory if you want. If this is a good spot in your life, why? Is it because your marriage is strong? Is your job going well? Are you close to your kids? Are your bills all paid? Do you have a hope and a future? Yes, you do, as a matter of fact, see Chapter Five.

7. Think about the memory of this special moment; but only the good things. You will almost always have some conflict or drama in the background – forget that right now and just focus on the good stuff. How old are you? What is the date? If you are watching your kids, how old are they? What do they like to do right now? What do they look like? What are they wearing? What do they sound like?

8. Go deeper into that memory if you want. If this is a good spot in your life, why? Is it because your marriage is strong? Is your job going well? Are you close to your kids? Are your bills all paid? Do you have a hope and a future? Yes, you do, as a matter of fact, see
 Chapter Five.

9. What are you thankful for right now?

Really soak it up and make the moment last as long as you can. We all need to go home sooner or later, so drink this memory with all you have so you can access it later!

To help you with this project, I'll give you an example. This is a short one but involves my wife, bike riding and a good dessert on a sunny day. Perfect.

June 14th, 2014. Our 16th anniversary.

We are young and in love and healthy. We spent the day riding bikes on Mackinac Island and enjoyed all the beauty of that place. It was warm and sunny and before we had to catch the boat back to the mainland, we had one more stop at the Iroquois Hotel.

We've stopped here before, but it was usually cold or rainy. Today it's perfect. We sat at a table with an umbrella outside on the patio overlooking the water.

We can see the tour boats coming and going into the harbor and the lighthouse out in the water. When we listen closely, we hear horses on the street behind us, clip, clop, clip, clop. We can also hear people on bikes and the occasional ringing of a bell.

We are splitting a famous "mile high lemon meringue pie," which is light and fluffy. There is shredded lemon on top of it and it melts in our mouths with each bite. We take small bites to make it last.

We are drinking ice cold water and it is refreshing going down. From here we can smell the fresh cut grass and, as usual, the horses in the street. It's okay; it's part of the character of Mackinac Island.

When we took the boat back, we saw an entire rainbow over Lake Huron and knew that God had good plans for our lives. Life is good.

Now it's your turn. Take some time with this. Sketch if you want or tape a picture here if you have one. Anything to help lock it in. Or do this in a sketch book or journal; but also, do it in your head because you might lose the journal or this book. The longer you make this description, the longer it will help you later. Go.

CHAPTER FOUR
ALL OF THAT FOR KIDS

What I'm seeing on Facebook is that kids of all ages are being affected by the bad news, not just adults. They don't understand why this is happening, and as a parent you might be reluctant to tell them the truth or even your version of it. Without getting political, people are dying. What kid would not be afraid of that? Even if that information is not the source of their anxiety or the reason they might be acting out or sad, many kids are lonely or bored.

Remember being bored? The same rules apply for kids—keep busy. In fact, most of these counterfeit depression solutions will help your kids too. It is up to you, Mom or Dad, to not freak out so they don't freak out and to walk them through this historic event. No pressure.

This morning, one of my nieces posted a drawing that one of her sons did of himself and the word *lonely* in the middle of it. Even with excellent parents and brothers and sisters, he doesn't understand why he can't play with friends or go for ice cream and why there is tension in the house that was never there before.

This is tough on kids. Help them understand that emotions are real and matter, then show them how to deal with them. See if you can text a friend, call a friend or write a note to a friend or relative. I'm sure Grandma or Grandpa would love to hear from them; I treasure those phone calls! Hopefully Grandma or Grandpa can make them laugh so you can all move on. Hey, have them draw a picture for Grandpa to use for a bookmark or for Grandma to hang on the refrigerator. The giving and showing of love will help.

As far as best memories, your kids might not even be old enough to have many good memories, so try this approach:

Ask them about their favorite memory and, depending on age, help them draw out the details. Have them think of a fun time they had and draw a picture of it or print a picture from the event. You can use it as a reminder of better times at bedtime and make new "best memories" as you do other fun or meaningful activities or vacations. You can also take a walk in the woods or watch some ducks or go see the baby lambs on a farm—it does not have to be Disney World!

When you are in the middle of making those memories, sit your kids down and tell them, "You know what? This day is so good we should remember it forever. Let's look around and notice everything we can!" You can do that using "I spy" if that makes it easier. Write it down someplace where you can find it in five years. You will be making a treasure book. If you have a great memory, frame it and hang it on the wall where they can see it when they are in bed.

Now folks, remember that if they are in one of "those" moods, they might not be able to think of a single good thing that happened in their life. True? You might need to prod them with your version of a memory.

Maybe you need to stop what you are doing and go make a memory right now. If nothing else, find their favorite toy and make up a story about it or look really hard in the grass for bugs or watch birds, and then make a memory out of that.

Assure them that this will all be over soon and then things will be better. Remember what I said – when you are having a really, really bad day, it MUST be better tomorrow.

CHAPTER FIVE
SWEET DREAMS

Let me start by saying that one of the common signs of depression is oversleeping; that is not what I am talking about here. If you just want to sleep all the time, either because you are always sleepy or because you honestly can't think of a reason to get up, you need to talk to somebody or your doctor.

However, since I firmly believe in the importance of taking naps and getting regular sleep, here are my tips for making that easy, even when you have a mind full of junk.

I realize you might have some serious things on your mind or trying to fall asleep on a hard surface, in prison, next to someone snoring or in a noisy place, so just do the best you can with what you have control over and you will find that you can do most of the things on this list.

1. Don't fill your mind with all kinds of junk like violent games, horror movies, or crazy TV shows full of blood and anger. Like I said before, GUARD YOUR PEACE.

2. Don't go to bed upset. Do your best to put your mind in a state of peacefulness. Some days I look forward to going to bed so much because it has been a hectic or rotten day. Sleeping is my comfort zone and moves me ahead to the better day I'm expecting.

3. Turn off the TV, quit the games, put down the book, and log out of Facebook, Instagram and whatever phone apps you are on at least an hour before heading for bed. Turn off the screens.

4. Make your bedroom a quiet place. We took the TV out of the bedroom so that room is just for sleeping and getting dressed. If you have a studio apartment, try not to watch TV, especially violent shows, from your bed. Do the best you can.

5. Next, turn down the temperature and close the blinds to make it dark if you can.

6. Get ready for bed. Brush your teeth, wash your face, and if you've had a hard day or worked up a sweat, take a hot shower and get clean, it helps a lot.

7. Now, slide into bed and soak up the feeling of the bed carrying your weight and the blanket and pillow making you more comfortable than you have been all day. Ahhh. If you dream, tell yourself you are going to have a great dream tonight.

8. Realize that no matter how much you fret over the frustrations that happened today, no matter how much you think about solving a problem, and no matter how much you want to replay or solve the problem you are feeling right now, it won't help you go to sleep.

   Let me say that in another way. Even if you figure out how you want to solve that nagging issue, it is *more than likely* that by morning you will have forgotten the brilliant solution or realize it was a stupid idea; moreover, if you happened to write it down, you probably can't read what you scrawled down anyway!

   So, forget trying to solve all the world's problems when you are trying to fall asleep.

9. If you are a person who always has a song in your head, think of your default peaceful song. My nighttime default song is "Give Thanks" or "Great is Thy Faithfulness."

This is where the best memories chapter comes in and the reason I asked you to get ALL the details.

> I hope by now you are starting to grasp my point that there are excellent benefits in being a Christian. You want to call it a crutch? I'll agree with that. We all have broken legs and I'm glad to have a crutch when I need it!

10. Pick one of your best memories and run it through your mind. If your mind wanders back to your problem, do your best to start over. If your mind wanders to another place or time and it's not painful, let it go there.

11. Think about what you are thankful for. What is the bright spot in your life? Is it your spouse or your kids? Is it a friend or your job? Maybe it's the food in your refrigerator?

12. Pray for your friends and family. To make this easy and to get you started you can do it alphabetically; like this for example:

A is for Amy – Lord, please bless her and give her favor and to find her way in the world where she can serve you and be a blessing to all the people she comes in contact with.

B is for Becky – Lord, thank you for an awesome wife and for her servant heart and desire to know you better every day. Bless her with health and strength.

C is for Chris – thank you for the good heart you put in him! Put people in his path who will help him understand your unconditional love and your purpose for his life.

David, **E**lizabeth, **F**aith…you get it.

13. Pray God's BEST for people. Do not only pray for the problems your family and friends are going through, but also pray a huge blessing over them. This one tip alone can yank you out of a feeling of depression because you are giving something so powerful to somebody else and not being selfish about it.

What does that sound like? My grandkids' lives are not written yet; when I pray God's best for them, it includes their health; that they would have great friends and would respect their parents and other authority; that God would show them their purpose and passion in life and give them overflowing hope, JOY and positive attitudes. I pray that their friends would be able to count on them; that they would grow up to be men and women of integrity. I pray that they would keep themselves free from any harmful addictions and would never suffer from severe sickness or accidents or spend a minute in prison.

For my grandsons, I pray that their future wives, who are just little girls now, would grow up with these same qualities and that they would find each other when the time is right. I pray that they would know, love and trust Jesus and seek His best for every area of their lives!

Then I pray for their parents for wisdom, guidance, health, prosperity and all the strength they will need to grow these kids up!

14. Go through the names or songs of God:

A – God you are awesome (think about that for a while).

B – Your name is beautiful.

C – You are the creator, maker of Heaven and Earth. Good job with the fish by the way.

D – You are my deliverer, my interceder in times of trouble.

E – You are El Shaddai – God with Us!

F – You are the Father, my "daddy" God!

G – You are good, all the time!

If you get stuck, move on. There may be a few letters that there is no description for, and you might need to do a Bible study to make this list, but that's a really good exercise.

15. These tactics don't always work. You might need to read (something peaceful) for a while or put on some soft music. Sometimes, like the day I started writing this book, you need to surrender and get your day going <u>with the understanding</u> that you might get some counterfeit depression in the form of sleepiness when you run out of steam later.

If you have other tips to fall asleep quickly, please let me know and write them here.

CHAPTER SIX
FINDING JESUS,
YOUR NEW BEST FRIEND

Wait, what? Keep reading...

If you want to throw this book in the fireplace because you are so sure God is a hoax and the Bible is a fairy tale, be open minded and see if this makes sense.

Remember what I was saying about "soul unrest"? Those things come from doing things you know are wrong; what we don't like to call sin.

> *For all have sinned and fall short of the glory of God.*
> *Romans 3:23 NIV*

Yes, all of us. Once you admit that, you can ask Jesus to forgive you.

> *If you declare with your mouth, "Jesus is Lord," and believe in your heart that God raised him from the dead, you will be saved.*
> *– Romans 10:9 NIV*

Like a lot of people who have been turned off by "you are a rotten sinner going to Hell" preaching, I have some good news for you. God not only has love, He IS love and only wants good things for your life!

The verse you probably know by now that is always at the football games in the end zones is John 3:16.

For God so loved the world that He gave his only begotten son, that whosoever believes in Him shall not perish but have everlasting life.
   -   John 3:16 KJV

That's pretty simple – just believe in Him and you get to go to Heaven? Yes, but the very next verse take the "you are all sinners" concept and add something important to it!

For God did not send his Son into the world to condemn the world, but to save the world through Him.   John 3:17 NIV

Hey, Pete, what's with the NIV and KJV? The Bible was written by 35 people over thousands of years in at least 3 different languages. It's amazing that it is one continuous story. To translate all of that into English took a bunch of scholars many years of work, with the King James Version (KJV) completed in 1388. Many, like hundreds of versions, interpretations and languages have been written since then. The NIV stands for the New International Version. It's very popular and easy to understand. By the way, when you plug in to a church, you might want to find out what version they prefer so you can be reading the same words.

Sorry, back to the story. Here is an illustration by Pastor Dave Cokonougher of the House of Prayer in Haslett, Michigan that I really like.

Imagine you and a friend have a big mud bog truck and you find a huge puddle of mud in your neighbor's field. Awesome, let's go, man!

So you are out there having a blast... and you get stuck. I mean, stuck up to the windows. You are sitting there trying to figure out what to do when you feel the ground shaking. You realize it is the property owner and you didn't get permission to be on his property. Great. Over the hill comes a huge tractor that can run right over your truck and finish driving you the rest of the way into the mud. We are in so much trouble.

When the tractor gets closer you can see the farmer and realize it's old man Jones and that's not a good thing. You don't dare jump out of the truck and make a run for it because it's up to your armpits.

But then...you see his face – and he's laughing, grinning and smiling – that's the face of LOVE and you know it's going to be okay. He came to yank you out!

God is the face of LOVE! We call him Father but he's not an earthly father, he's a perfect Heavenly Father – he only wants good things for his kids.

Are you ready now to make Jesus an important part of your life?

Just pray this simple prayer out loud:

> *Jesus, I know that I'm a sinner and can't save myself. I'm sorry for my sins. I trust you to forgive me and save my soul. Jesus, I confess right now that you are the Lord of my life. I believe God raised you from the dead. I open the door of my heart and ask you to come and live in me and I'll live for you. I will seek your will for my life. Thank you for saving me! Amen.*

Done. Your sin calculator has just been cleared and you have a brand new life. Write the date here:

Now what?

- Tell somebody you just accepted Jesus as your LORD.

- Read your Bible (or download the free YouVersion app). Start in the book of John if you don't know where to begin. The entire Bible is also a history book, so some year read the whole thing, it's pretty fascinating; and it is documented, not a fairy tale.

- Get involved in a Bible believing church or find one online, though it's not the same, and make some great friends. If you know somebody who is always talking about their great church, ask them about it.

- You will know when you find your new church home by the welcoming handshake at the door and the loving, smiling interactions between the people who go there.

- Keep in mind that we all have our own struggles and none of us, including the staff, are perfect. For a lot of us, our church is our second family and we want you to be a part of the family. Search for preaching you understand, but if you have questions, ask a leader to help you find answers. Some churches have more basic teaching on Sunday and deeper preaching on Sunday nights; find out what is available and where you fit in at this point in your walk with the Lord.

Onward!

Before I forget, I have used the term God and Jesus but there is a third part named Holy Spirit. You may have heard of them as Father, Son and Holy Ghost. One God, 3 forms, kind of like H2O – water, ice, steam. One H2O, different forms. That's the best I can do to explain it in my simple (not God) mind. The study of them is another book but I can sum it up this way:

Father, Son and Holy Spirit were all there in the beginning (Genesis). God made a covenant, like a contract, with a man named Moses. Well, Moses kept his part of the deal so for God to keep his part of the deal, he sent His son Jesus to Earth. When Jesus left, he sent Holy Spirit to be our helper, our power and our Joy.

CHAPTER SEVEN
FEAR – THE OPPOSITE OF FAITH

Depression and those feelings we described in Chapter One are not JOY. Not only that, you will never find joy in a new car, new shoes, candy, a drink, a fat bank account, a video game or a really great vacation.

During this COVID-19 event, Joy might be especially hard to find because there is so much *fear* coming at us from all directions – and so many versions of what the safe thing to do is; should you stay at home or is it okay to go to the park? It's okay to take a canoe out, but not a motorboat (Michigan); you can buy paint at Ace Hardware, but not at Home Depot; should you wear a mask or not?

Of course, we want to be safe in these days, and if you are infected or at risk, quarantine yourself; the rest is just plain FEAR.

FEAR is the opposite of faith.

So how do you build your faith? The Bible has the answer for that:

> *So then, faith cometh by hearing, and hearing by the word of God. – Romans 10:17 KJV*

By the way, I mention the book of Romans a lot because it has given me so much hope over the years. It's a book that Paul wrote from Corinth to the church in Rome.

On the first day of a horribly painful divorce, I got to spend a night in jail to cool off. Good thing I had been in a Bible study of the book of Romans and had this weapon to help me through the night:

> *And we know that in all things God works for the good of those who love him, who have been called according to his purpose. – Romans 8:28 NIV*

Notice that verse does not say that everything will work out for everybody. In my simple mind I picture God up there moving pieces around on a chess board so I can win because He loves me so much; I'm sure that is not the way it works. I have been told that God watches our lives as if He's standing on top of a building watching a parade. He can see the beginning of the parade way over to His right, He can see us in front of Him and He can see the end of our life coming down the road. Time is not the same for God.

Anyway, it took a few years but, yes, God did replace everything I lost in the divorce with something better. There were plenty of times I wanted to quit and move away or worse, but God saw me through. He will also see you through, but God won't force you to do anything; most of your life is up to you.

If you are having thoughts of suicide or homicide, don't give into those thoughts – never give up. Get some help.

> **The National Suicide Prevention Line**
> **1-800-273-8255**
>
> If you prefer to chat with them, search "suicide hotline" and you can find a live link there, every day, day or night.

Oh, and by the way, God does not make bad things happen in your life. Those rotten parts come from the devil.

> *The thief comes only to steal and kill and destroy; I have come that they may have life and have it to the full.*
> *– John 10:10 NIV*

So, let's move on to that full life!

CHAPTER EIGHT
COMFORT AND SECURITY

Before we get to Joy, let's stop for a minute and talk about God's promises for comfort and protection. These are more things you can think about to battle depression and fear.

If you've ever been to a funeral, you have probably heard of "The 23rd Psalm." It's a song written by the second king of Israel, King David. He wrote it during his darkest time. His forces were fighting a civil war. The other side was led by his son, Absalom.

Before David was king, he was a shepherd, so he used references to the animals that had to depend on him for everything. It's a great Psalm for tough times.

Here it is:

> *The LORD is my shepherd, I lack nothing. He makes me lie down in green pastures, he leads me beside quiet waters, he refreshes my soul.*
>
> *He guides me along the right paths for his name's sake.*
>
> *Even though I walk through the darkest valley, I will fear no evil, for you are with me; your rod and your staff, they comfort me.*

You prepare a table before me in the presence of my enemies.

You anoint my head with oil; my cup overflows.

Surely your goodness and love will follow me all the days of my life, and I will dwell in the house of the LORD forever.

Psalm 23
NIV

Right after the Twin Towers in New York fell on 9/11/2001, I started hearing about Psalm 91 and how people had memorized it and were "mysteriously" late for work or somehow spared the day at the office. I had read Psalm 91 but never heard of the hope it gave people in the protection God offers to those who trust Him:

Whoever dwells in the shelter of the Most High will rest in the shadow of the Almighty.

I will say of the LORD, "He is my refuge and my fortress, my God, in whom I trust."

Surely he will save you from the fowler's snare and from the deadly pestilence.

He will cover you with his feathers, and under his wings you will find refuge; his faithfulness will be your shield and rampart.

You will not fear the terror of night, nor the arrow that flies by day, nor the pestilence that stalks in the darkness, nor the plague that destroys at midday.

A thousand may fall at your side, ten thousand at your right hand, but it will not come near you. You will only observe with your eyes and see the punishment of the wicked.

If you say, "The LORD is my refuge," and you make the Most High your dwelling, no harm will overtake you, no disaster will come near your tent. For he will command his angels concerning you to guard you in all your ways; they will lift you up in their hands, so that you will not strike your foot against a stone. You will trample the great lion and the serpent.

"Because he loves me," says the LORD, "I will rescue him; I will protect him, for he acknowledges my name. He will call on me, and I will answer him; I will be with him in trouble, I will deliver him and honor him.

With long life I will satisfy him and show him my salvation." Psalm 91 NIV

Wait...doesn't the Bible say, "in this world you will have trouble..."? Yes, it does. But to quote the whole verse changes everything. It actually says:

I have told you these things, so that in me you may have peace. In this world you will have trouble; but take heart, I have overcome the world. – John 16:33 NIV

As you spend time reading the Bible, you will find yourself more and more hopeful and joyful. Remember, faith comes by hearing and hearing by the Word. If you are confused, get a study Bible to help you understand the nuances and the original meaning of the text.

One of the most encouraging authors is Joyce Meyer. Her best-selling book, "Battlefield of the Mind," has changed lives for 25 years.

If you are struggling with fear and depression, study the Bible for encouraging passages, write them down and put them in places you can see them – like on your dashboard or your bathroom mirror. There are plenty of verses that touch on a variety of life issues, such as salvation, answered prayer and praise, prosperity, making wise decisions, your family and marriage, the power of your words, love, tithing and giving. I have put 24 of my favorite verses in the end of the book for you to cut out and memorize. Those are your spiritual swords!

CHAPTER NINE
FINDING YOUR JOY

JOY is very important to the quality of your life. Joy is worth finding because it lets you ride through the tough times, gives you hope when there is none, and lets you walk with a smile on your face that is contagious to your family and everybody you come in contact with during your day.

Since we started with writing a description of depression, let's try the same thing with Joy.

- Joy is happiness, but better.

- Having joy is having a smile on your face.

- Joy is a feeling that all is well at that moment in your life.

- Joy is knowing that whatever rough time you are going through will eventually get better.

- Joy is better than contentment.

- Joy is more than peace.

- Joy is the feeling you get when you wake up excited to start another day.

- Joy is a feeling of well-being.

When I Googled *Joy,* I found:

- A feeling of great pleasure and happiness.

- Joy is an attitude or belief, which soothes even in the most sorrowful of situations. Joy comes from within; it is an internal view. Joy in the Biblical context is not an emotion; it is not based on something positive happening in life but is an attitude of the heart or spirit. (https://healthpsychology.org)

Make finding JOY one of your life goals, something on your bucket list. It will take work and require some changes to your thought life.

JOY comes from inside you, so you need to:

1. Change the stuff you put into your head. It's the classic "garbage in, garbage out" argument. If you want joy, you need to turn off violent, angry shows and walk away from situations that trigger negative emotions. Get rid of addictions that steal your joy like overworking, porn, drinking, drugs, gossip, etc.; replace it with uplifting books, movies and shows that don't put more fear into your heart; study the Bible. Seek JOY.

2. Change the things you think about. Don't dwell on past hurts or grudges; replace it with prayer for others. Think of good things you can do for other people and ways you can bless them with words of kindness and encouragement, gifts, or volunteering with worthy organizations.

3. You might need to change the people you listen to and spend time with. You might need some new friends who encourage you, believe in you, and tell you the truth.

4. You need to develop new, healthy habits for your body. Get more fresh air, eat better, and exercise more; even something as simple as taking the stairs.

5. Get rid of all regrets, unforgiveness and negativity.

6. If you are experiencing grief, set a time limit.

7. Use your life to help others. It does not have to be going on a mission trip to Africa. Be kind, open doors for people, and help when you see an opportunity.

8. Become generous with your time, talent and treasures. Do this without expecting anything in return.

9. Learn to be content, not always striving for the next shiny thing.

10. Learn to be thankful, regardless of your circumstances.

Please understand that any one of those things could be its own book, but it does not have to be that complicated.

The Bible recounts many celebrations that include the phrase "there was great joy." There are hundreds of verses in the Bible that talk about Joy or rejoicing; *that's* a good study. Below is a sample of the verses referring to joy.

Many of the Psalms have words of encouragement for those who need it.

> *You make known to me the path of life; you will fill me with JOY in your presence. – Psalms 5:11 NIV*
>
> *The precepts of the Lord are right, giving JOY to the heart. The commands of the LORD are radiant, giving light to the eyes. – Psalms 19:8 NIV*
>
> *The Lord is my strength and my shield; my heart trusts in him, and he helps me. My heart leaps for JOY, and with my song I praise him. – Psalms 28:7 NIV*
>
> *You turned my wailing into dancing; you removed my sackcloth and clothed me with JOY. – Psalms 30:11 NIV*

Clap your hands, all you nations, shout to God with cries of JOY. – Psalms 47:1 NIV

Shout for JOY to God, all the earth! – Psalms 66:1 NIV

Those who sow with tears will reap with songs of JOY.
– Psalms 125:5 NIV

Deceit is in the hearts of those who plot evil, but those who promote peace have JOY. – Proverbs 12:20 NIV

Jesus brought JOY to the earth even before he was born. When Mary's cousin Elizabeth, who was expecting her son John the Baptist, heard Mary come into the room, she said:

As soon as the sound of your greeting reached my ears, the baby in my womb leaped for JOY. – Luke 1:44 NIV

Maybe you remember these words, made famous by Linus in *A Charlie Brown Christmas*:

> *And there were shepherds living out in the fields nearby, keeping watch over their fields at night. An angel of the Lord appeared to them, and the glory of the Lord shone around them, and they were terrified. But the angel said to them, "Do not be afraid. I bring you good news that will cause great JOY for all the people. Today in the town of David a savior has been born to you; he is the Messiah, the Lord." – Luke 2:8-11 NIV*

They were terrified. Understandable. But that same Jesus is still alive and giving JOY today!

Ultimately, finding JOY is a decision.

The Apostle Paul was a man who understood joy. You can read his story starting in Acts Chapter 7. While Paul was preaching all over the Roman empire, he was shipwrecked, beaten to within an inch of his life, thrown into jail several times and ended up dying in Rome.

But he had JOY. Here's what he said about it:

> *In all my prayers for all of you, I always pray with JOY. – Philippians 1:4 NIV*

> *Then make my JOY complete by being like-minded, having the same love, being one in spirit and one in mind.*
> *– Philippians 2:2 NIV*

Even his guards noticed something different about Paul:

> As a result, it has become clear throughout the whole palace guard and to everyone else that I am in chains for Christ. And because of my chains, most of the brothers and sisters have become confident in the Lord and dare all the more to proclaim the gospel without fear. – Philippians 1:13-14 NIV

See, JOY is contagious, and it should be in your life too. They say that yawns are contagious, and we know that laughter makes everybody in the room laugh; joy is the same way. When you walk into a room, take your JOY with you and show people some love. When you leave the room, somebody should feel better because you crossed their path.

Be so full of JOY that you overflow to those around you!

The following verses are for you to cut out and put in places where you will see them everyday such as on your mirror, dashboard or refrigerator. The Bible calls scripture the Sword of the Spirit. There is other armor that you can "put on" every morning too. You can read about it in Ephesians, chapter 6.

The Lord is near to all who call upon him, to all that call upon him in truth. He will fulfil the desire of them that fear him: he also will hear their cry, and will save them. Psalm 145:18,19 KJV	He will call upon me, and I will answer him; I will be with him in trouble, I will deliver him and honor him. Psalm 91:15 NIV
Even though I walk through the valley of the shadow of death, I will fear no evil, for you are with me; your rod and your staff, they comfort me. Psalm 23:4 NIV	The Lord is my light and my salvation; whom shall I fear? The Lord is the stronghold of my life; of whom shall I be afraid? Psalm 27:1 NIV
I sought the Lord, and he answered me; he delivered me from all my fears. Psalm 34:4 NIV	He who dwells in the shelter of the Most High will rest in the shadow of the Almighty. I will say of the Lord, "He is my refuge and my fortress, my God, in whom I trust." Psalm 91:1,2 NIV
So do not fear, for I am with you; do not be dismayed, for I am your God. I will strengthen you and help you: I will uphold you with my righteous right hand. Isaiah 41:10 NIV	And we know that in all things God works for the good of those who love him, who have been called according to his purpose Romans 8:38-39 NIV

You, dear children, are from God and have overcome them, because the one who is in you is greater than the one who is in the world. 1 John 4:4 NIV	For God did not give us a spirit of timidity, but a spirit of power, of love and of self-discipline. 2 Timothy 1:7 NIV
Because your love is better than life, my lips will glorify you. I will praise you as long as I live, and in your name I will lift up my hands. Psalm 63:3-4 NIV	Praise be to the Lord, to God our Savior, who daily bears our burdens. Psalm 68:19 NIV
Finally, be strong in the Lord and in his mighty power. Put on the full armor of God so that you can take your stand against the devil's schemes. Ephesians 6:10 NIV	..but those who hope in the Lord will renew their strength. They will soar on wings like eagles; they will run and not grow weary, they will walk and not be faint. Isaiah 40:31 NIV
Commit to the Lord whatever you do, and your plans will suceed. Proverbs 16:3 NIV	For I know the plans I have for you, declares the Lord, plans to prosper you and not to harm you, plans to give you hope and a future. Jeremiah 29:11 NIV

Peace The Lord gives strength to his people; the Lord blesses his people with peace. Psalm 29:11 NIV	**Comfort** He heals the broken hearted and binds up their wounds. Psalm 147:3 NIV
Comfort I will turn their mourning into gladness; I will give them comfort and joy instead of sorrow. Jeremiah 31:13 NIV	**Peace** Peace I leave with you; my peace I give you. I do not give to you as the world gives. Do not let your hearts be troubled and do not be afraid. John 14:27 NIV
Holy Spirit But the fruit of the Spirit is love, joy, peace, patience, kindness, goodness, faithfulness, gentleness and self-control. Against such things there is no law. Galations 5:22-23 NIV	**Anger** In your anger do not sin: Do not let the sun go down while you are still angy, and do not give the devil a foothold. Ephesians 4:26-27 NIV
Depression/Loneliness Do not be anxious about anything, but in everything, by prayer and petition, with thanksgiving, present your requests to God. And the peace of God, which transcends all understanding, will guard your hearts and minds in Christ Jesus. Philippians 4:6-7 NIV	**Depression/Loneliness** Humble yourselves, therefore, under God's mighy hand, that he may lift you up in due time. Cast all your anxiety upon him because he cares for you. 1 Peter 5:6-7 NIV

Made in the USA
Monee, IL
30 June 2020